T0194905

Greater than the Dark

1 John 4:4

Written & Illustrated by Kay Waugh

WESTBOW
PRESS®
A DIVISION OF THOMAS NELSON
& ZONDERVAN

My first book is dedicated to my first born, Samara. Samara was my only child for close to six years before her brother came along. She prayed for a sibling and got one. For the past 4 years, Samara has exhibited patience (although difficult at times), tenderness and love so beautifully despite the struggles life has thrown our way. These reflections of goodness are not her own but a reflection of Christ's tender mercies and lovingkindness. I need her every day to show me glimpses of the Father's heart to remind me I need to continuously work on my own. May we all be inspired to reflect the Father's heart to those around us, to bless them. May we all draw near to Him & thank Him for all our many blessings. May we aspire to be vessels whom the Father uses to manifest heaven on earth. I love you Samara, more than mere words could ever explain. I can't even explain how much you've taught me, how much you've been refining me just by being you. The world so desperately needs more tender-hearted and caring children like you.

You made the moon to mark the seasons,

and the sun knows when to set.

You send the darkness, and it becomes night,

when all the forest animals prowl about.

Psalm 104:19-20 NLT

There's a time of day when things dim to grey,
birds begin to settle down doing the
last of their flying around.
The world gets quiet amongst the chirps and sings,
landing in their nests to fold up their wings.
Flutter, flutter, flap, flap, don't worry Samara,
tomorrow morning they'll be back.

Can you fold up your wings?

"What happens at night when
I go to bed?" said she-
looking up at her mom ever so nervously.
She wondered and gasped at what could be said
all the while curling up her toes in bed.

Can you curl up your toes?

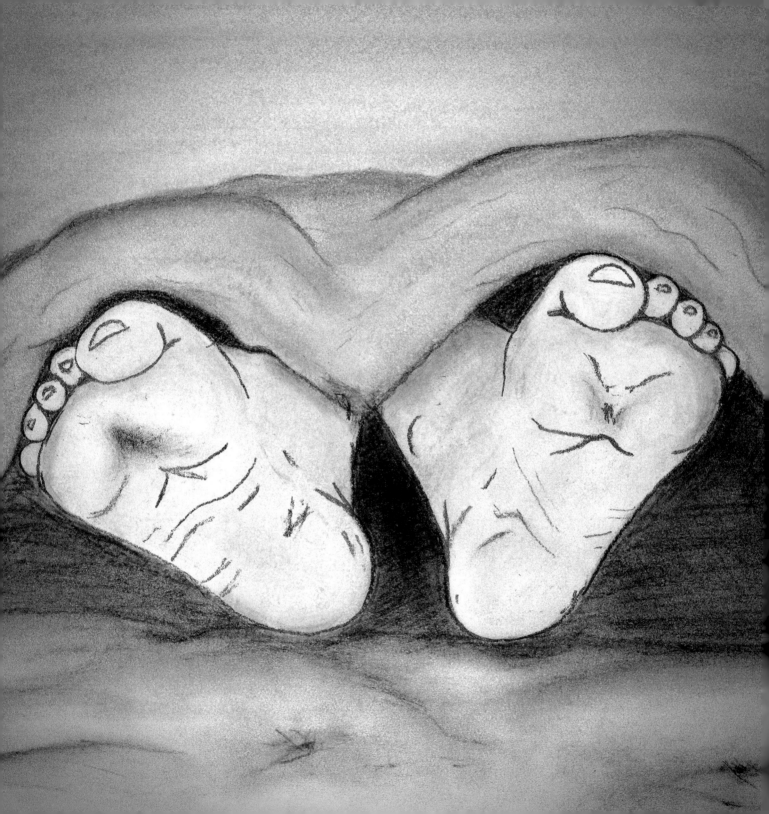

"Let me share with you the truth
of what goes on at night,
it won't give you a scare, it will give you delight."
Mommy knew what to tell her little curly one
and that she'd be calmed once she was done.

Make a calm face like the hedgehog.

"Night time is when many feel afraid
of the shadows, coos and noises made.
The sun goes down so some start to fear
forgetting that there is always a Light near."

What kind of sounds do you hear at night?

"Things get dark and there are
strange sounds to be heard
but what scares most is when it's
silent- not a peep- not a word.
Nightfall is when critters bustle about
because for them it's their morning
so they want to get out!"

Can you stretch like the skunk?

"They scamper about trying not
to give people a fright-
quietly starting their day, softly
with all their might.
Owls have it worst of all, no
matter how hard they try
people think they are frightening and
startle when they take to the sky."

Make your best owl sound.

"What if I told you there was
One far beyond the skies
who created everything, cannot do
wrong and never tells lies.
What if I told you this One is God who made
the heavens and earth as it should."
"Now God saw all that He had made, and
indeed it was very good." {ISV*}

These truths are found in Genesis 1:1,
*1:31 as well as Psalm 146:6

"The earth was once formless, once dark
but His Spirit changed it with an instant spark.
His Spirit was over the waters then He
commanded, 'Let there be light.'
He saw that it was good to separate day
from the darkness we call night."

Read Genesis 1:1-5

CRASH! BANG! BOOM!

Samara yelped, "Mommy what's that sound?"

"Its hungry animals seeing if

there is any food around-

look out your window it may be a raccoon or fox.

See- there's a mommy with her

babies sniffing around the box."

How many raccoons do you see?

"Samara, God is Maker of everything,

even the dark belongs to Him*.

Creator of all things good, not of evil, or sin.

'The everlasting God is your place of safety.

His arms will hold you up forever.'**

So my darling, you belong to God, not fear

because His Spirit within you is greater."***

Read *Psalm 24:1, **Deuteronomy
33:27 ICB and ***1John 4:4

"When you doze off your body grows, nature
rests, the animals eat- don't you know?
They aren't afraid of what scares you so.
They have peace within the darkness
because they have big eyes to see
that twilight is made for us to
enjoy, not feel scary."

"Don't be afraid of what comes
once the sun goes down,
He is Lord of all, most greatly renown.
He is in charge of the the weather, the
seasons and all that scurries about.
This should fill your heart with
joy- not worry or doubt."

Read Psalm 74:16 and find the animals.

"God also uses bedtime in a special way to talk to us through dreams. He spoke to many like Jacob, Samuel, Joseph with help from His special teams. Angels stay awake with God, **never sleeping, always on the watch**. At the sign of anything wrong they are ready to help, ready to launch." *

Read about the angels in *Psalm 91:11

"Even Jesus used sunless times to pray,
the disciples would wake up to find Him
doing so at the start of the day.
Also, did you know, the tomb was dark
when Jesus rose up from the grave?
He had no fear because He conquered
the darkness to save."

"Jesus is the Light of the world, there is a
way to carry Him in your heart you see.
All you have to do is ask Him to
live there for now and all eternity.
Memorize promises found in the Bible
then the darkness fades real fast.
Any fears or imaginations become
a thing of the past."

Read about Jesus, the Light of the world in John 8:12

The Lord Himself will go before you.
He will be with you.
He will not leave you or forget you.
Don't be afraid. Don't worry.
Deuteronomy 31:8 (ICB)

"God only ever gives good things
so memorize His Word.
It is filled with treasures to erase
all fears that are absurd.
God did not give you this spirit that makes you
afraid, He fills you with His power, love and peace!
So in Jesus' name we command all
fear, worry and panic to cease!"

Memorize 2Timothy 1:7 & Deuteronomy 31:8

"Sweet dreams" Mommy said.

"Now it's time for lights off- I'll tuck you in bed."

"Mommy," Samara gently spoke, "I hope I
dream of a snuggly koala in Noah's Ark,
I'm not afraid anymore because my
God is greater than the dark!"

With that, Samara let out a loud breath and smiled,
feeling safe in her heart because
she is Jesus' child.
Mommy closed the light then gently tucked her in,
fluffed her pillow folding the
blanket up to her chin.

Can you let out a breath and smile?
Can you fluff up your pillow?

Mommy added, "Remember Psalm 3 verse 5,
it will put your heart at ease
yet make you feel alive,
'I can lie down & go to sleep- I will wake
up again because the Lord protects me.'"
Suddenly, Samara was fast asleep
dreaming ever so peacefully.

Hey Kids! Ask Jesus to be Lord of your
heart- to make it pure, make it clean.
Ask for forgiveness, mean what you
pray and the changes will be seen.
He loves us no matter what & He
promises to take away your fear,
the world can't offer you this, a
better deal- there is none my dear!

My Letter to Parents

Anxiety can be summarized as a gripping, consuming fear. A seven letter word only scratches the surface of the dreadful torments one's mind and body goes through while experiencing anxiety. Thankfully, my daughter doesn't have a severe fear of the dark- but I did! Fear and anxiety is something I still battle with even now as an adult. As a child, even with a nightlight I was anxious and afraid. I have now discovered the Key to overcoming the fear of all darkness. I have come to know the Ultimate Nightlight, the Light that "shines in the darkness, and the darkness can never extinguish it" John 1:5 NLT. My Nightlight is the very Light of the world (John 8:12), the Word of God. Your children are never too young to learn or to hear about God's powerful Word. His Word is the only weaponry, only artillery, only thing that will never fail, never disappoint! This Word is living, powerful, active, alive (see Hebrews 4:12) so sharing it with our children is the most important legacy, the most important gift, to ever give them for it is the very source of life itself! You must be the one to teach your children to be a light (Matthew 5:14), not a flickering, weak, dim one but a strong, beaming light that the darkness cannot comprehend (John 1:5). It all starts with you- the only way to effectively do this, dear parents, is for it to START WITH YOU! Have your own personal relationship with Christ. Have daily devotionals with your kids. It is the greatest investment you can ever make. I recommend reading the story and if time permits, look up the verses afterwards. School, TV or activities won't feed their souls, just going to Sunday school and mentioning Jesus once in a while won't do it either, the key is: lifestyle! As a family resolve to have a Christ-centred lifestyle every day! I prayerfully encourage each and every one of you to pick up your Bible and use it to charge up your light to overcome all fear, overcome any worry. Use verses as ammunition for every subject and occasion. Fight fear with the facts of His Word, it guarantees you, anxiety will subside, and your children will no longer be bound by fear (Galatians 4:7). Take charge parents! "Put on salvation as your helmet, and take the sword of the Spirit, which is the word of God." Ephesians 6:17 NLT

Printed in the United States
By Bookmasters